The Florida Evergl[a]

Contents

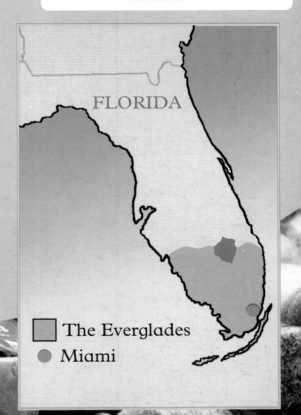

FLORIDA

☐ The Everglades
● Miami

What Is the Everglades?

The Everglades is a low, flat plain. In the wet season, it becomes a wide, grassy river, and the grasslike plants seem to go on forever. That's why it's called the Everglades!

The Native American name for Everglades is *Pahayokee*, or "grassy waters."

The Everglades carries water from central Florida to the Gulf of Mexico. This water gives life to the communities of plants, animals, and people along the way.

Everglades National Park is just 40 minutes by car from downtown Miami.

Animal and Plant Life

The Everglades is much more than a water marsh. It has a number of very different habitats, each with its own unique plants and animals.

Marine

Florida Bay

Mangrove swamps

Winding rivers where fresh water from the Everglades mixes with salt water from the Bay

Coastal prairie

Dry, windy, and salty with low growing dese[r] plants

Slough

The deeper center of the wide, marshy river

Pinelands

Dry, rugged pine forest

Hammocks

Islands of junglelike trees growing in the middle of the slough

5

Many species of beautiful birds once lived peacefully in the Everglades. Then in the 1800s, it became fashionable for women to wear hats made with large feathers. Thousands of birds in the Everglades were killed, and many species were in danger of becoming extinct.

Many of the feathers used in hats were from the snowy egret and the great egret.

In 1905, the Audubon Society hired game wardens to protect the birds' breeding colonies. Later, laws were made to protect the birds.

The pink feathers of the roseate spoonbill were also popular.

Alligators dig out plants and mud in shallow water to create alligator holes. During the dry winter season, these holes are sometimes the only places where there is water. Often, other animals that live in the area move in with the alligators. Some of these animals will become winter meals for the alligators, but without the alligators, none would survive the dry season.

The Everglades is the only place in the world where the alligator and the crocodile live side by side. How can you tell an alligator from a crocodile?

	Alligator	Crocodile
Color	Blackish (adult)	Olive brown
Snout	Wide	Narrow
Teeth	When jaws are closed, upper teeth can still be seen	When jaws are closed, upper and lower teeth can still be seen
Nest	A mound of plants made by the female in freshwater environments	Mud or sand in brackish or saltwater environments
Status	At one time endangered—now making a comeback	Endangered—only a few hundred remain in the United States

A Park in Trouble

The Everglades is the only ecosystem of its kind in the world, but it wasn't until the early 1900s that people began to appreciate how special it is. Ernest F. Coe and others worked to have Congress pass a bill to protect the area. Finally, on December 6, 1947, President Harry S. Truman dedicated Everglades National Park.

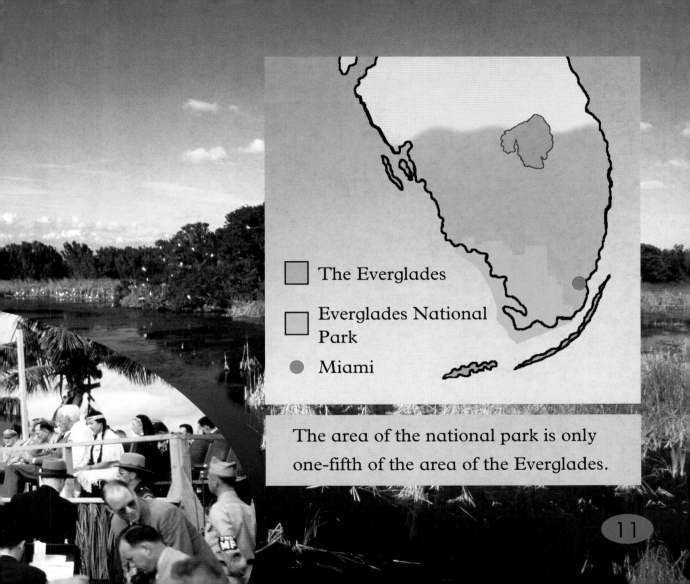

The Everglades

Everglades National Park

● Miami

The area of the national park is only one-fifth of the area of the Everglades.

Park Facts

Land Area	1.5 million acres
Number of Plant Species	150 species of trees and treelike plants
Number of Animal Species	More than 40 species of mammals About 350 species of birds More than 50 species of reptiles 18 species of amphibians
Number of Endangered Animal Species	15
Number of Threatened Animal Species	6
Number of Visitors Per Year	About 1 million
Activities for Visitors	Wildlife viewing, fishing, boating, canoeing, hiking, bicycling, boat tours, tram tours, camping

A big problem facing the Everglades is loss of habitat. Early settlers thought the Everglades area was a worthless swamp, and they began to reclaim the land. Between 1905 and 1910, large areas of wetlands were drained to make farmland. By the 1920s, new towns grew as more and more people moved to the area.

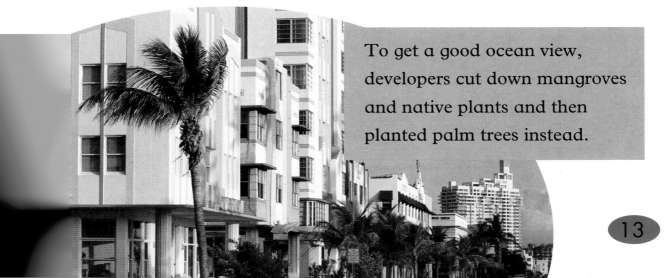

To get a good ocean view, developers cut down mangroves and native plants and then planted palm trees instead.

When cities grow, they build over natural habitats. One of the animals that has lost most of its habitat as a result is the Florida panther. It once lived throughout most of the southeastern United States, but a study in 1990 found that there were fewer than 50 Florida panthers still surviving.

Many panthers have been killed by speeding cars on highways.

Another animal affected by the loss of its habitat is the crocodile. In 1975, it was declared endangered and thought to be the rarest reptile in the United States. Special areas in Florida Bay were set aside as crocodile sanctuaries. Now, after 30 years of protection, the news is good. The American crocodile population seems to be on the increase.

Another big problem facing the Everglades is changes to the water flow. The Everglades has a natural cycle of six months of summer rains and six months of a dry season.

Every day, 900 people move to Florida. This means that every day the demand for water grows by 200,000 gallons.

This cycle is necessary for the survival of plants and animals in the Everglades that are adapted to the alternating seasons. But people are affecting this natural cycle.

The area around Lake Okeechobee in central Florida used to become flooded in the summer, which would create a river that flowed south through the Everglades. Today, people control how the water in the river flows into the Everglades. More than 1,700 miles of levees and canals wind through South Florida, moving the water first to farmland and towns and finally to Everglades National Park.

Lake Okeechobee

Fort Lauderdal

agricultural area

Miami

If too little or too much water is released through the floodgates, it can cause a disaster. Wading birds feed in shallow water, using their bills to hunt for small fish. If too much water is allowed to enter the park, these birds can't find food for their young. Up to 300,000 wading birds used to nest in the Everglades. Today, fewer than 15,000 still nest there.

endangered
wood stork

Alligators build their nests on high points of land to ensure that their eggs are not washed away during summer rains. But if people release too much water into the park during the nesting season, the nests are flooded and the eggs are destroyed.

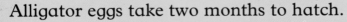
Alligator eggs take two months to hatch.

The Effects of Farming

Farming has also affected the Everglades. Lands once flooded by the Kissimmee River have been turned into pastures for cows. One cow can create as much waste per day as 20 people. Farmers also use fertilizers and pesticides, which run off into the water and contaminate it.

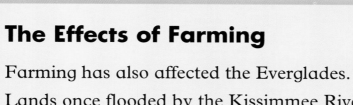

Restoring the Balance

People once thought that national parks were safe and would be preserved forever. We now know this is not true. National Parks are not cut off from the rest of the world. Whatever happens outside the park has an impact inside the park too.